LAILA LAUSON

THE STAR INTERVIEW

The Ultimate Guide to a Successful Interview,
Learn The Best Practices On How to
Ace An Interview As Well As Crucial Mistakes You Need
to Avoid In Order To Land the Job

Descrierea CIP a Bibliotecii Naționale a României
LAILA LAUSON
    THE STAR INTERVIEW. The Ultimate Guide to a
Successful Interview, Learn The Best Practices On How to Ace
An Interview As Well As Crucial Mistakes You Need to Avoid
In Order To Land the Job / Laila Lauson. – Bucharest: Editura
My Ebook, 2020
    ISBN 978-606-983-610-1

LAILA LAUSON

THE STAR INTERVIEW

The Ultimate Guide to a Successful Interview,
Learn The Best Practices On How to Ace
An Interview As Well As Crucial Mistakes You
Need to Avoid In Order To Land the Job

My Ebook Publishing House
Bucharest, 2020

CONTENTS

Quick Start Job Guide 7

Resumes 9

Functional Resume Example 14

The Job Hunt 19

Networking 25

The Interview 33

Typical Interview Questions 36

The Day of the Interview 41

Sample Thank You Letter 45

Conclusion 47

Quick Start Job Guide

Anyone that has looked for a job in today's society will tell you that it is not an easy task. For every job opening that is available, there are hundreds of applicants trying to get the position.

In this ocean of job hunters, it is easy to become overwhelmed and discouraged by trying to obtain a job. To be able to make it to the top of the applicant pile and get the perfect job, youneed to know the keys to landing any job.

The keys to are the tools that will set you apart from any other person seeking the same jobs that you are.

Most job hunters just apply to a job opening and expect to get the job.

In today's world that is simply not going to happen.

There are many steps that need to be taken by anyone interested in landing a job. The steps are simple and when applied to every job hunt and application will help you to land the perfect job. The steps that you need to take as you try to land your next job are the keys to you job hunt success.

From the time that you decide that you want to get a new jobto the moment you accept the job offer, you will be working the steps that will make you successful in your endeavour.

It is important to follow these steps for every job search thatyou can embark on. The sections of this book are laid out so that they follow the process that you will take to land your next job.

You can also use this book as a reference tool along the way of your job search. Refer back to the sections of the book thatyou need to work on as often as you need to.

There is no right or wrong way to use the information contained in this book. **The only mistake that you can make when job hunting is to not use the steps to achieve your success.**

The biggest thing that you need to know as you try to land the perfect job is that the only thing that can hinder your success is you. People who choose to not take the appropriate steps, will not see the success that they want. You now have the keys to your job-hunting success in your hands.

Now it is up to you to use these steps to help you succeed and land the perfect job.

Resumes

Types of Resumes

When it comes to applying for jobs, your resume is the first chance that you have to make a first impression.

This is the single document that will get your foot into the door for you to take the next step.

A great resume will get you to the top of the applicant pile. The first step that you need to take is to choose the type of resume that you will write for yourself.

All resumes are not the same basic template and you need to be aware of this before you write your resume.

There are four types of resumes that you can choose from, **chronological, functional, combination, and targeted.**

Functional

If you do not have a lot of work experience, you may want to choose a functional resume. This type of resume is a great way to focus on the skills that you have that would help to distinguish you from the other applicants.

This resume will focus on your skills rather then your work experience. You may want to choose the functional resume if you are changing careers or you have large gaps in your employment history. This is also a good type of resume to use for first time job hunters.

Chronological

A chronological resume is the most common type of resume that people use. This resume lists your work history first.

The list of your jobs starts at your most recent and working your way back through the rest of your jobs. It gives employers a glimpse at your work history. This is why this is one of the most popular types of resumes with recruiters. The chronological resume gives them you work history at a quick glance.

Combination

The combination resume is a way to combine the parts of a functional resume and a chronological resume. This type of resume lists your skills and experiences first.

The next part to this resume is a list of your work history in reverse chronological order. This resume helps you to highlight skills that you possess that will get you the job that you are applying for, while showing your work history as well.

Targeted

The final type of resume is the targeted resume. This resume is the most difficult type to use because you need to update it for each individual job that you apply for.

In a targeted resume, you showcase the skills that you have that are relevant to the position that you are applying for.

For each job that you apply, you will need to change the skills that you focus on.

Sample Resumes Most Common Types

Chronological Resume Example Paul Smith
123 Main Street

Any Town, SA 12345 555.555.5555 (home)
566.486.2222 (cell)

psmith@email.com

Experience

Manager, House of Wigs April 2001 - February 2005

- Opened new location
- Placed orders to restock merchandise
- Managed payroll, scheduling, reports, email, inventory, and maintained clientele book and records
- Integrated new register functions
- Hired and Trained Staff

Sales Associate, Wigs R Us July 1999 - April 2001

- Merchandised wigs
- Set-up displays

- Worked with clients to get repeat business
- Scheduled private shopping appointments with high-end customers

Sales, The Pantry House February 1997 - July 1999

- Provide customer service in fast-paced atmosphere
- Maintain and restock inventory

Education

State College, Any Town, State

Computer Skills

- Proficient with Microsoft Word, Excel, and PowerPoint, and Internet

Functional Resume Example

John A. Allan

123 Simon Street, Any City, Pa 11111 Phone: 555-555-5555

Email: jallan@email.net

OBJECTIVE

To obtain a position where I can utilize my skills with management skills, organizational, and sales skills.

Summary of Qualifications

Results oriented, hands on manager with a high level of results oriented work done in the retail fashion industry with experience in handling high volume stores.

Major strengths include great time management, ability to lead by example, problem solving skills, and a desire to succeed.

Personal Accomplishments

Expert in human resources and recruiting. Hired and trained staff for 7 new locations.

Education

Bachelor's in Fabric, State University, Any Town, State

References

No matter what job that you are applying for the prospective employer will want to see professional references.

The norm is to have at least 3 references available to give when you apply for a job. The references need to be of a profession not personal nature.

This means that your references should be people that you have worked with and not family and friends. In today's work field, it is often hard to get professional references.

Many jobs tell employees that they may not give references to people that have worked for them. There are ways to get references.

There are coworkers and supervisors that you are working with that will ignore the rules and give you a reference. You need to be discreet when you ask them to do this for you.

Make sure that you are willing to do the same for them if they should need references at some point. It never hurts to ask someone to see if they would be willing to be one of your references.

You can ask people that you have volunteered with to be your reference. These people have seen your work ethic and can talk about your time management and dedication to what you are doing.

These are great attributes for a reference to be able to speak to.

If you do not have a previous job to go back to for references, you can always use people in your schooling. You can ask teachers and counsellors in your school to be a reference for you.

The most important thing to remember when making a list of references is to ask the person that you want to use first. You need to ask people before you list them as a reference for your new job.

This way they will be expecting to hear from jobs that you are applying to. When you finally get the perfect job, make sure that you send thank you notes to all of your references to thank them for the help that they gave you.

Printing and Presentation

Now that you have your resume and references written, you are not done. You still need to print them out and have them ready to give to the jobs that you are applying for.

There are a few options that you can use to have your resume look professional.

You can take your resume and references to an office store and have them printed out from a flash drive. The printers that office stores use are a high quality and will make your resume look great as it is printed.

The workers at the store can show you the correct paper for them to print out your resume on. This takes a lot of guess work out of printing out your resume, but it will cost you extra money.

You can print your resume at home. Make sure that your printer's ink is full so that you have a clean and crisp print of the document.

You will need to purchase a high quality paper that is of a heavier weight then common copy paper. You can find this paper for sell any place that sells office supplies. It is usually labeled as resume paper. It is best to use a white or cream colored paper.

Print out many copies of your resume and references. You will always want to have at least 4 copies of both in your brief case as you go out to talk to prospective employers. It is better to have more copies of your resume on you then you will need then to run out.

There are also several reputable online services that will help you create and publish the most professional resume template possible.

Here are a few of my personal favorites:

http://resumizer.com/ http://www.niceresume.com
http://www.pongoresume.com http://skillcraze.com/

Extra Tips:

Use a laser printer.

Use high-quality stationery.

Print your resume on cream or ivory-colored paper, of at least 24 pounds in weight.

Avoid heavy paper, which can crease and damage the print.

The Job Hunt

Once you have your resume completed, the real challenge begins. The job of finding the perfect job for you, yes, looking for a job is going to be like already having a job.

This is a process that takes dedication to the time involved to be successful. You will need to dedicate time each day to looking for jobs to apply to.

To get the perfect job, you need to find it first. The best way to do this is to dedicate a set amount of time each week to your job search.

One of the best time frames is to set at least 8 to 10 hours a week. Schedule this time into your daily calendar. This is time that you must put into your job search.

People who say that they cannot find a job, are the ones that have not invested the time in looking for one. The perfect job is not just going to land at your feet. You will need to look for it.

This will take time.

Often times, you will not know that the job that you are looking at is the perfect job. That is why you will want to devote the time to finding many jobs to apply to.

Doing this will take time and effort. This is why you need to look at the search for a job as your part time job. By giving your job search this type of dedication. You will be successful in finding and landing the perfect job.

Where to Look

There are many options of where to go and what to do to find a job. The old way of walking door to door to businesses and asking whether they are hiring a thing of the past.

Now you can do a lot of your job searching from the comfort of your own house. But, even with staying at home there are many options for your job search to look at to help you find the perfect job. Every job search option has its good points and badpoints.

Online Job Search Sites

The world has gone the way of the Internet when it comes to job searching. Online job search sites have become one of the most popular options for job seekers everywhere. There are many different online job search sites out there, monster and career builder are two of the most popular.

There are numerous pros to using online job searching sites. One of the biggest pros is that there are numerous jobs listed on one site. This will save you a lot of time in your job search. By typing in a few keywords about the job that you are looking for, you will be able to bring up hundreds of jobs that you can apply to.

Another pro to online job sites is that prospective employers can find you as well. You do not always need to find all of the job openings yourself.

When you post a profile to an online job site, you can make your resume searchable by prospective employers. By doing this, you may have the perfect job end up coming to you.

Not all is perfect in the world of the online job sites. There are cons to this method of job hunting.

One of the cons is that you are competing against hundreds of other job applicants for every position that you apply to. Because the sites are so popular, there are millions of people that log on each month to search for jobs in this method.

Another con to using the online job search sites is that it is hard to customize your application to each job. On these sites, you upload one resume and one cover letter.

These are the things that you use to apply to all job openings on their web site. Since you upload one resume and cover letter to use, it is very difficult to personalize each application that you send out in the hopes of getting a job.

Here are a few places to begin your search:

http://www.Monster.com http://www.jobbankusa.com
http://www.jobopenings.net/ http://promotions2.workopolis.com
http://www.careerjet.com/ http://workbloom.com/

Newspapers

One of the tried and true ways of searching for a job is with the newspaper want ads. In the movies, you will see the person that is job-hunting sitting at their kitchen table circle newspaper ads for a job.

This is a very good visual of a way for you to look for a job. All you need is your highlighter and a copy of your local newspaper to get started on this job hunt.

Newspapers have been around for a long time and so have their want ads. Many business owners feel more comfortable looking for job applicants through the newspapers.

These business owners shy away from the Internet as being a risky way to look for new applicants. There are many jobs available through the newspapers that you will not find online. This is a great advantage in the world of job hunting.

One of the cons for newspaper ads is that the application process for many of these jobs can be much longer then their online counter parts.

The problem with applying to ads through the newspaper is that you will usually need to fax or drop off your resume.

Many companies that use newspapers ads still place resumes into a database so that they can search for keywords from possible applicants.

This means that once your resume is received, it must be entered into their computers. This will take more time then an online application.

Here is a very handy resource that feature thousands of online newspapers (updated daily):

http://www.onlinenewspapers.com/

Networking

One of the least used resources for a job hunter is networking. Classes and books talk about using networking to find great job leads. They are right.

To find the perfect job, you will want to do some networking. Networking is talking to people in the field that you are looking to get a job in to find out about job leads that they may know about.

The biggest reason that you will want to use networking, as one of your job-hunting resources is that you will hear about job openings that are not advertised. Many of the best job openings never get posted to job boards.

The companies tell their employees about the job opening. Someone that the employees know will fill the position. The general public will never be aware that the job opening existed. This means that you will have little to no competition for the job.

The hardest part about networking is knowing the right people to get the job you want. You may not know anyone working in the field that you want to work. This will make networking difficult for you. It is hard to know about the best job openings when you cannot be looped into the grape vine about them.

Job Hunting By the Numbers

Job hunting can be looked at just like sales. Any salesperson will tell you that sales are a numbers game. This is also true for job hunting.

When it comes to looking for a job and applying you need to play by the numbers. You will not land every job that you apply for.

It is for this reason that you need to think of everything that you do as an investment into your final success.

Most job hunters will only hear back from about 30% of the jobs that they apply to. This number may seem low to you, but is an accurate average of the rates of return on job-hunting. Out of the number that you hear back from, you will go on the interview. Of the interviews that you go on, you may get a job offer from about 10% of them.

Here is the Breakdown

Resumes Sent Out 100 Interviews 30
Job offers 3

Now your return numbers will fair better then the average from using this process to get the perfect job. This is only a reminder that you need to apply to many jobs to land the perfect job.

Cover Letters

A cover letter is the document that you send along with your resume, to introduce yourself to prospective employers. Many employers will choose to skip over resumes because of the lack of a well written cover letter.

No matter what type of job that you are applying to you needa well written cover letter.

You can look at a cover letter as someone introducing you to speak in front of an audience. It is one short page to introduce yourself and give a brief highlight of your skills. This is the place where you can convince the prospective employer to look over your resume.

Many job hunters choose to write one cover letter and use it for every job that they apply to. This is not in their best interest to land the job. A form cover letter will read just like a form letter.

The hiring manager at the company that you are applying to, will not like the same cover letter being sent to every job opening.

They want to see effort and creativeness put into the cover letters that they receive.

That having been said. You can use a cover letter template and then customize each cover letter to the job that you are applying to. This will set your cover letter apart from the rest and get you the job interview.

To be able to customize a cover letter template you are going to need some basic information about each job. One of the best practices of job hunting is to keep a copy of the help wanted ad that you are applying to. This will be a vital piece to refer to often as you prepare to apply to the job.

One of the pieces of information that you will want to have is where you saw the company's ad and when. Many employers want to know which of their recruiting techniques are working.

Another piece of information that you will need from the help wanted ad is the list of qualifications. You will choose one to two of the qualifications that you are going to focus on in your cover letter. In the letter you will point out how your skills match these two qualifications.

The third piece of the cover letter information that you need is the name of the position that you are applying for.

This company may have many job openings that they are recruiting for. Make sure that they know what position that you want to be considered for.

If there is the name of a contact person on the help wanted ad, you will want to note this. It is better to address your cover letter to a specific person when you can. This will help to give your cover letter the feel of being individualized.

After you have used all of the information that you have gotten from the help wanted ad to write your cover letter, there is one vital point left to make.

You need to ask for an interview. This may seem like it is something that goes without saying.

This is not true. You need to make the point of asking to be called to set up an interview.

Make sure that you give contact information in your cover letter. The times that you are available to take a phone call is a great way to help the prospective employer get in contact with you.

You will also want to list your phone number in the cover letter as well.

Cover Letter Template

Your Name Your Address
Your City, State, Zip Code Your Phone Number
Your Email Address Date

Employer Contact Information

Name Title Company Address
City, State, Zip Code

Salutation
Dear Mr./Ms. Last Name:

Body of Cover Letter

This is where you will use all of the information that you acquired to ask to be considered for the position that you are applying.

This is one the first steps to selling yourself to get the perfect job

Complimentary Close: Respectfully yours, **Signature:**

Handwritten Signature (for a mailed letter) Typed Signature

Do not use the terms in bold from the template on your cover letter.

Application Process

As you begin to apply to the jobs that you have found through job hunting, you may begin to feel overwhelmed. You need to apply to many job openings to get the perfect job.

Because you are applying to many jobs, you need to stay organized with your job hunt. This organization will help you to succeed and get the job that you want.

One of the most important ways to stay organized when you are applying to jobs is to follow the same process every time that you apply. This will help you to get into a routine as you apply to the many jobs that you have found.

Follow whatever instructions may exist on the help wanted ad on how the employer wants you to apply to their job opening. Thisis a very important indicator to prospective employers about whether you can follow directions.

Some companies may want you to email them your resume as a word attachment.

Some will want you to cut and paste your resume into the main email. Another option that some companies use is that they will prefer you to apply directly through their web site for all job openings.

Do whatever the company that you are applying for requests.

After you have applied to the job, you will want to follow up with the employer. This is a way to check and make sure that they received your application and to check on the status of it.

The best time frame to wait for the follow up after sending in an application is a week. This will give the company time to look over your application. You can do this follow up through a phone call or email.

To make sure that you keep track of all the applications that you send out, it is good to use an application-tracking sheet.

Nothing is worse then receiving a call from a possible employer to set up and interview and you cannot remember applying to them.

A tracking form will also help you to track you follow up dates after you apply and after your interview.

The Interview

Your resume was stunning. Your cover letter caught the attention of the hiring manager and moved your application to the top of the pile. You have landed one of the most coveted things on the road to landing the perfect job.

You have an interview set up!

Hold On! Just because you have gotten an interview, does not mean that you work is over on the road to getting the job. **This is the time when you will need to put forth the extra effort** to keep your name above the rest of the applicants when it comes to the job.

Hiring managers place their decision to hire someone for an open position almost entirely on the interview. This is the make or break part of the process to get the job. One false move and you will be back at the starting point scratching your head, wondering where it all went wrong.

Do not worry there is a way to make sure that you achieve success on your interview. Interviews are a basic part of the job search. There is a process to follow when it comes to interview, just like there is a process to follow when it comes to the other steps of landing the perfect job.

Preparation

Before you head out to an interview, it is important that you fully prepare for it. You will want to take these steps for every interview that you go on.

By preparing for job interviews, in advance you will help your success. This preparation should start a couple days before your actual interview.

It is important to research the company that you are interviewing with before you go on your interview.

The interviewer will ask you questions to see how well acquainted with the company that you have applied for. This will show the interviewer that you are truly interested in the company.

By doing the research, you will also know if you are truly interested in working for this company.

One of the things that you will want to do before the day of the interview is to take a dry run to the place of the interview. This is very important especially if you have never been to the company that you are interviewing with.

Drive to the company at the time that you would for the interview. This will give you an idea of what type of traffic you will hit on the way. You will also feel more comfortable and at ease the day of your interview by already knowing the lay of the land around the company.

Another step in the preparation process for the interview is to read over commonly asked interview questions and have your answers already planned out.

Most interviewers use the same questions and differ from the normal questions almost never. This makes it easy for you to know how you will answer almost any question that is given to you. This will help to keep you sounding assured of yourself.

By knowing what is going to be asked and having answers already planned out, you will be able to keep your nervousness to a minimum.

Typical Interview Questions

Tell me a little about yourself.

This is not an open question to go into every little detail about your life. You need to keep your answer to this open-ended question very professional. You will want to give a 1 to 2 minute summary of your professional life.

Describe a typical workday for you.

This is where you will want to highlight the skills that you use in your current job that will be beneficial to the job that you are applying. You want to make your day sound interesting and full of challenges that you meet and solve.

Why are you leaving your job?

This can be a tricky question for many job hunters. If you are changing careers, you may want to highlight some of the reasons that you are changing industries.

Answers that will work for many interviews is that you are looking to work closer to home and that you are looking for a company that you can grow with. One of the answers that you do not want to use is that you are looking for more money.

What is your best and what is your worse attribute?

Answering the first part of this question is often easy for most people in an interview. It is the second part that gives people trouble.

You need to say that something about you is bad, but you do not want the interviewer to see you in a bad light.

One of the best answers to the worse attribute is that you are a perfectionist and that you will keep working on a project until you get every little detail right.

What interests you about the job?

This is where some of your research will come in handy. You can point out how some of the responsibilities that the employer listed in their want ad are items that you have wanted to work with.

You can also point out that the company is at the cutting edge of your profession and that you want to grow with an industry leader.

Attire

There is a type of dress code when it comes to a job interview. There are dos and don'ts when it comes to what to wear.

Many times the first impression that you make with the clothing that you wear to an interview is the most important.

You will never get a second chance to make a first impression.

It is better to over dress for an interview. If you are truly unsure of what type of dress is expected at a job, it is better to dress your best for an interview.

This means a suit and button down top. This basic interview outfit will be overkill for many interviews.

The upside to choosing this tried and true look is that you will look pulled together and there is no way that the interviewer will think that you are under dressed.

There are many interview situations that do not require a suit. Many jobs are more casual then a suit and there for you can dress down a little bit.

For men, a button down shirt and tie with a nice pair of dress pants are ok for a more casual interview. Women can pair a nice blouse with dress slacks or a skirt.

The most important thing to remember when choosing an interview outfit is to make sure that you err on the conservative side. Tops should not be low cut and skirts should be no shorter then knee length for women.

For men, you will want to keep the color choices for your outfit on a muted scale.

All interview outfits should fit you well. An ill fitting interview outfit shows the interviewer that you do not take the time to make sure that your clothes fit. They will wonder if you willtake the time to make sure that your work has no errors.

You also need to make sure that your interview clothes are pressed and wrinkle free. This will give you a clean crisplook.

You hair should be neat and tidy. Any makeup that you wear should be subtle and understated. Perfume and cologne should be skipped on the day of the interview.

You want to make sure that your accessories do not make an impression for you. You want to make sure that the interviewer is concentrating on what you have to say and not on what you are wearing.

It is a good idea to have 2 to 3 interview outfits that you can go to. Many jobs require more then one interview. You will need to have different outfits for each interview that you go on. Set these outfits aside in your closet so that you know they are what to wear to an interview.

What Not to Wear

Sweat pants Jeans Sneakers
Open toe sandals Flip flops Sleeveless tops Low cut tops
Clothing with stains and holes

T-shirts Baseball hat Sunglasses
Workout clothing Shorts
Skirts shorter then knee length Lots of jewellery
Perfume and cologne Bright makeup

The Day of the Interview

The day of the interview, you will want to get dressed and pack your briefcase for the day.

Inside your briefcase, you will want to place 3 copies of your resume and two copies of your references. Other items that may come in handy are a couple of pens and a pad of paper to write information down on.

Leave for your interview earlier then you think you need to. The last thing that you want to do is to be a late for a job interview.

Punctuality is one of the most important qualities that employers want in their employees. The best way to make a good impression at a job interview is to arrive 15 to 20 minutes early.

Walk into the company and ask for the person that you will be interviewing with. Many times the interviewer will ask the person that you approached about you. You will want to make sure that you give this person a good first impression of you as well.

When you meet the person that you will be interviewing with, you will want to look them in the eye. Greet the interviewer with your best smile and a handshake.

Follow the interviewer to the place that you will be having the interview at.

Take the seat that the interviewer offers you. If you are wearing a coat, you will want to drape the coat on the back of the chair so that it does not get in the way during the interview.

Place your briefcase on the floor at you feet.

Sit up straight in the chair with both feet on the floor to givethe best impression in your interview.

Smile as you answer the questions that you are asked. Maintain eye contact with your interviewer. Interviewers are taught that a lack of eye contact is a sign of a person lying to them. Do notlet your nervousness make it look like you could be lying.

Try to answer the questions posed to you within 20 seconds of being asked. This will show that you are well prepared for this job interview.

At the end of the job interview, shake your interviewers hand and thank them him for his or her time. You should ask for the interviewer's business card as you leave. This will help you when it comes to sending a thank you note to your interviewer.

Follow Up

Follow up after your job interview is very important to ensuring that you are offered the job. The interviewers will be seeing many applicants over the time that they are looking to fill inthe job opening.

There are two steps to the follow up process that you will needto follow to ensure that your name stays in the interviewers mind.

The day that you come home from the interview, you will wantto write a thank you letter to the interviewer. It is important to thank the interviewer for their time and consideration on the position that you were applying for. Mail the letter out the next morning to the interviewer.

The next step to the follow up to your interview is a follow up call. Many interviewers will give you an idea about when a decision will be made concerning the open position that you applied for.

If your interviewer did this, you will want to use that time line for when to place a follow up call. When there is no time frame as to when the decision will be made, it is best to make your follow up phone call two weeks from the day of the interview.

When you place the follow up phone call to the business that you interviewed with, you will want to ask for the person that you interviewed with. Introduce yourself, tell him that you had an interview with him, and give the date.

This will help to refresh his memory of whom he is talking to. At this point, you will want to ask about the status of the open position.

You will hear two answers.

One answer is that the position has been. The better answer is that they are still interviewing.

You can choose to ask the interviewer when they hope to make their final decision. As you wait for your job offer, continue to go on interviews and follow the process.

Never count on getting any job until you have received the call extending an offer of employment to you.

Sample Thank You Letter

Your Name Your Address
Your City, State, Zip Code Your Phone Number
Your Email Date

Name Title
Organization Address
City, State, Zip Code Dear Mr./Ms. Last Name:

Use the first paragraph to thank the interviewer for taking the time to meet with you on the day of your interview. You need to mention the position title that you talked about in the interview

The second paragraph gives you another chance to sell yourself for the position that you interviewed for. Use examples of what the job position requires you to do to highlight your strengths.

This is a place to make the point that you are the person thatwill be the perfect fit for the company and the position

In your closing paragraph, thank the interviewer again for his time and consideration. Reiterate your interest and excitement about the position that you applied for. Close your thank you letter by telling the interviewer that you look forward tohearing from him soon.

Sincerely, Your Signature

CONCLUSION

Landing the perfect job isn't an impossible task, however it does require patience and commitment.

If you put in your best effort, and you are persistent in your search for a high paying, flexible job that you would enjoy waking up to every single day, you will succeed.

Remember, it's important to prepare for each interview ahead of time. Never leave this until the last minute. Have a friend or family member brief you, by literally sitting down and conducting a 'mock' interview. This experience will help calm you and give you a boost of confidence for when it's time for the real, face-to- face, event.

Take a deep breath, plan out your schedule and get moving! To your job seeking adventure (and ultimate success),

Your Name,
Your Domain Here

www.ingramcontent.com/pod-product-compliance
Ingram Content Group UK Ltd.
Pitfield, Milton Keynes, MK11 3LW, UK
UKHW022213230426